How

How To Quickly Pro
Skier To Conf

Contents

Introduction

Hello and welcome to; *"How To Ski: How To Quickly Progress From Beginner Skier To Confident At Skiing"*. This is my second book in a bestselling series designed to train you for the slopes without needing to rely on expensive and often frustrating paid instruction or multiple ski vacations per year.

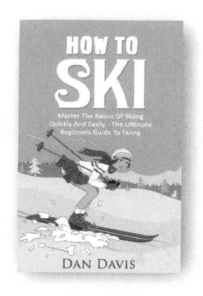

Hopefully, you've already read my beginner's book to skiing and learned a great deal from it, finally gaining the confidence to give skiing a try. If you haven't already seen this book, I'd suggest that you go back and explore everything that it has to offer as it is so thorough and provides that essential background that you need to build upon if you want to improve. You can get a copy at the following link: **https://www.amazon.com/dp/B014HRUKSI**

But worry not- you can still boost your ski performance and overall confidence with me right here and now even if you learned what you already know elsewhere, or even several years ago. Perhaps you're feeling rusty or are reticent to throw money away on expensive ski lessons. This book is designed to be a stand-alone resource for anyone who dreams of taking their skills to a bright new level and I'm pretty sure that this means you.

What To Expect

Let's be clear on one thing; this book won't have you competing in the next Olympics nor tackling those double-starred trails overnight. This is about getting to a place where you feel entirely comfortable and 'at home' on a pair of skis, strong, supple and ready to take on the world. You'll no longer feel like a klutz whose feet and legs seem to have life of their own, but sleek, controlled and almost-professional. Take a moment to imagine now just how that would feel.

Confidence is one of the core elements that will enhance your progression and skiing prowess tenfold, so that you can become the kind of sportsperson you dream of becoming.

How We Will Achieve Success

In this book I will show you just to how to gain that kind of supreme confidence and skill on the slopes by looking at every aspect of your performance from a biomechanics perspective, including positioning, nutrition, strength and flexibility and even precise muscle group training so that you will become a force to be reckoned with.

There's no time to waste- let's get right to it and see how we can catapult your skill to a whole new level. Come with me to find out how.

Chapter 1: Understand Ski Biomechanics

The first question on your lips right now is probably 'what the heck is ski biomechanics and what can it do for me?' In which case, you'll be very pleased to know that I'm about to explain it all to you right away. You'll learn how it is the most fundamental approach that will help you to reach a whole new level on the slopes and tackle almost any trial or gradient. An understanding of ski biomechanics facilitates the learning process, and is the secret that will take you from being an intermediate to a pro. Let's find out more.

What Is Ski Biomechanics?

Ski biomechanics isn't as complicated as it might sound. It's the science concerned with the internal and external forces acting on your body, and the effects produced by these forces. It's the real science of skiing and encompasses everything from applied physicals, fluid dynamics, psychology, nutritional science and materials science to optimize your fitness and performance. In essence, it helps you to understand the finer details of the ski experience, and will help take your skiing to a whole new level as it did for Olympic pro Steven Nyman[2].

Why Use Ski Biometrics?

It's quite likely that up until this point, you've been relying on feel and intuition to take you down the slopes safely. This is a fantastic approach to take and shows that you are getting more in touch with the skiing experience as a whole, and not just a set of techniques. So far, this has probably been working really well for you.

But to give yourself that extra 'edge' that you are seeking, you'll need to push ahead and consider the finer points of skiing to really progress.

Our Approach

Clearly, we don't have a ton of top-class instructors and therapists within reach along with high-tech wind tunnels and the like. But we can still get some outstanding results by paying the right degree of attention to the smaller details such as psychology, nutrition, fitness and technique.

Despite what you might be thinking, focusing in this way won't take any of the fun out of the equation- you'll still look forward to your two weeks on the slopes, or even more if you're really lucky. What it will do is inject that extra knowledge that will allow you to unleash all of that supreme skill when you do finally hit the slopes. And as a result, you'll have a whole lot of fun.

First we'll tackle the basics of posture and technique in a handful of straightforward steps so that you can hit the ground running. Are you ready? Let's go.

Chapter 2: Work On The Basics: 10 Tips For Success

When we are looking to improve our skiing prowess, it's easy to believe that we need to put ourselves through our paces and tackle all of the complicated slopes, training techniques and approaches. We believe that only by pushing ourselves hard can we achieve what we dream of.

Way back when I first started to learn, I thought exactly this and spent hour upon hour of training off piste and on, training, exercising, and doing everything that I believed would make a difference. Yet nothing seemed to. I still seemed to struggle with the same old issues, and whilst all of my sweat and tears paid off in other respects, nothing seemed to make much of a difference. Until I invested in several trouble-shooting sessions with a top-class instructor. I couldn't believe the difference, and I wished that I'd have taken the time to get it right from the start.

By just streamlining my posture, tightening certain core skills and paying attention to the basics, I had it all made.

You don't want to make the same kind of mistakes as I did. You don't want to waste months or even years of struggling when a handful of tweaks will make all of the difference. For that reason, this chapter is dedicated to streamlining the most basic postural issues. It's all wrapped up in a list of ten easy tips you can implement anywhere, whether you're in the comfort of your sitting room, the gym or right out there on the slopes. There's no time to waste- let's get to it.

1. Relax your toes

Many of us carry a great deal of tension in our toes, believing that this helps us when it comes to controlling our skis. But the reverse is actually true. The looser your toes, the better you can absorb variations in the terrain, stay upright, and stay in control.

2. Flex your ankles

The secret to better balance lies in flexing your ankles as well as your knees. In tandem, this keeps your body more upright and responsive to the terrains and shape of the trail.

3. Position your shins

You'd think where you have your feet make the difference in your ability to turn, but it's actually your shins. When you keep them right against the tongues of your boots, you'll find it easier to initiate those turns, your weight will be more centered and you will find a great degree of overall control.

4. Use your ski tips to turn

Do exactly this. To start a turn, put pressure on your ski tips and then let your feet follow.

5. Roll your skis

A common mistake is to flatten your skis between curves. Don't do it. Instead, roll your skis immediately into the next turn. This will improve your control and fluidity and reduces your chance of falling.

6. Keep your skis parallel

Both of your skis should work in parallel at all times. They should enter each turn precisely together and roll on edge simultaneously.

7. Keep your eyes forward

Good balance isn't only the rest of placing your limbs correctly, but from your entire body. I often see many beginners falling in the trap of looking in all directions, yet wonder why they end up falling so frequently. The trick is to keep your eyes forward. In addition to helping to maintain your balance, it will also boost your reaction time and allow you to focus on the experience as a whole.

8. Hands forward

Perfect hand posture is also really important for balance and control. Keep them forward, as if you're holding a tray of food in front of you.

9. Place your poles carefully

You can even tweak your pole placement to get some great results. Plant it to the side of the ski, instead of forward and you will notice an improvement in your rhythm, confidence and overall performance.

10. Center your weight

At all times, keep your weight in both feet and center yourself as much as possible. Keep your feet hip width apart. This will help you stay balanced and make you less likely to fall.

By perfecting these ten simply tweaks, you will develop the confidence and ability to tackle the most challenging of terrains. Keep yourself centered, balanced, eyes forward and position yourself accurately to instantly become more of a pro.

Now that we have targeted these very basic things, we can move forwards and explore the most detailed factors that will supercharge your performance. First we'll start with food and explore how nutrition can fuel your body throughout the day, keep the effects of high altitudes at bay and prevent muscle aches, pain and damage. Additionally, any injury will be far less likely to happen. Let's take a look.

Chapter 3: Eating For Performance: Ski Nutrition

When you're poised to hit the slopes and have an action-packed day ahead of you, you're going to want to fuel your body as well as your possibly can. Neglect to do this and you'll find yourself crashing and burning when your energy reserves run low, suffering more injuries and aches and pains and also find yourself more susceptible to altitude sickness. Doesn't sound like much fun, does it? Nor does it feel particularly professional to feel drained and wiped out after a session.

So what we need to do is get you fuelled correctly so you can take on those diamond trails with absolute ease and feel tired but happy at the end of the day. This chapter will fill you in on everything you need to know to do just that.

Eat more!

Skiing wipes a good chunk of calories off your daily intake; you burn around 300-600 calories up to around an intermediate level, and beyond that, you might even burn up to 1000. And these figures are per hour. Imagine how many hours you spend en piste and you'll begin to understand just one of the reasons why eating right is so vital.

All you need to do to remedy this is to eat more!

But don't think that this is an excuse to stuff as many burgers, cookies, chips and donuts down your throat as you possibly can. If you know anything about eating well, you'll know that this is always a bad idea.

Think whole grain carbs, lean protein, healthy fats and plenty of fruits and veggies and you'll be good to go.

Start Your Day Right

Make sure you eat breakfast if you want to perform at your best. You've been fasting for many hours overnight, so you need an injection of that all-important fuel to kick-start your metabolism, ignite your brain and wake up your muscles.

Oats, porridge and muesli are all superb options as they give you the healthy fats, and whole grains that your body most needs. Include a piece of fruit and you have the kind of breakfast that leaves athletes proud.

Even if you really aren't a breakfast person, make it your priority to eat something no matter how small. Even a slice of toast, a piece of fruit or a healthy grain bar will make a difference.

Snack Regularly

In order to keep your energy levels high, you'll need to keep eating throughout the day. Aim to eat healthy snacks that combine good levels of protein and carbs. Trail mix, healthy grain bars, nut butter sandwiches and bananas all work well. Just be mindful of the weather conditions outside when you pack- you don't want to rely on a banana and find that it has frozen solid when you want to tuck in.

Lunch

You've got the day off to an outstanding start- now it's time to relax, recharge your batteries and refuel your body before you head back out there again. Stick with the healthy carbs, lean protein, healthy fats and fruits and vegetable combination and you won't go far wrong. Round the meal off with a small piece of fruit such as an orange or a banana and you will feel unstoppable.

Dinner

It can be tempting to really let your hair down when your day has come to a close and you are feeling exhausted but happy. Don't feel too guilty if you surrender to the call of richer cuisine or something that you simply fancy- you will burn the extra calories off anyway, and a small indulgence every now again doesn't do too much hard long-term.

But you and I both know that you'll perform at your best if you keep your diet on track. Make it your mantra- 'healthy carbs, lean protein, healthy fats and veggies'.

Stay Hydrated

Being at such a high altitude can be really tough on your body, reducing your performance on the slopes significantly and increasing your risk of muscle damage. Yet drinking enough fluid is the simple trick that you can do to undo most of the harm and become even more fantastic than you already are. Did you know that a tiny 2% reduction in hydration[1] can have a damaging effect on what you are capable of at any given moment?

The moral of the story is, drink more water. Just do it!

Skip The Junk Food

Junk food is empty calories. Yes, it will provide energy that you need, but at what cost? These foods which are usually high in fats, sugars, and all kinds of other chemical nastiness will do great damage to your body if you let them. Plus, they lack that all-important nutrition that will power your adventures on the slopes, prevent you from suffering muscle damage, keep the effects of altitude at bay, and also keep you performing at your best. Skip the comfort food and do your body a favor.

When you really get in tune with the needs of your body, and really start to pay the attention it deserves, you'll be astounded by the transformation in your skiing prowess. Eat well, snack often, nourish your body with a good balance of the right food groups, hydrate and steer clear of junk, and you feel focused, energized, and ready to take on the world!

As you saw in the introduction, our overall mental state and confidence plays a huge role when it comes to performing at your best, whether this is on the ski slopes, or even in the rest of your life. Sadly, many of us lack confidence when it comes to practicing a new activity and fear can prevent us getting to the level we dream of. The next chapter will show you how to brush off your fear and effortlessly discover that supreme confidence you're after. Let's find out.

Chapter 4: Boost Your Confidence And Self-Belief

Let's be honest here- skiing is bound to evoke fear in a huge number of us human beings. You see, although under control, we are for all intents and purposes sliding down a mountain at great speed. Our survival instincts tell us that this might not be such a good idea, and may do what they can to protect us, even when it isn't entirely necessary.

So we feel scared.

And I'll be honest with you, I grappled with a huge amount of fear when I hit the intermediate stage like you. Somehow, I'd managed to escape it as a beginner, but suddenly, now I was able to control myself at higher speeds and on more challenging trails, I felt the fear unfold.

There were many days that I get that butterflies feeling in my stomach and almost dreaded hitting the slopes, despite the exhilaration I'd feel. And I knew that as long as I felt like this, I could never really improve my skills on the slopes. I could try, by all means. But unless I could give it my all, I'd never excel. I knew I had to do something.

This chapter, I'll will show you why fear was such a massive obstacle when it came to my ski performance and how it's holding you back right now. Then I'll explain a handful of effective techniques that I've tried myself and can vouch for. Let's take a look.

Why Fear Zaps Performance

Fear is your worst enemy when it comes to performance. When you are feeling fearful, your body is in overdrive. Your stress hormones are fluctuating rapidly, your heart beat is accelerated, blood is flowing away from your limbs towards your core and you are ready for fight or flight. If you are in this agitated state, there's no way in the world you can be focused and in control enough to ski safely and skillfully.

Surrender To Physics

I like to give my students the following analogy. Imagine you walk into the sea and stand waist-deep close to the shore. The current pulls your body, the waves crash into your torso and you are at the water's mercy to a certain degree. If you stand there rigid and inflexible, you'll soon find yourself overwhelmed by the chaos of nature around you. But, if you allow yourself to soften, to surrender to the sensation and to allow yourself to adapt to your surroundings in a fluid way, you'll feel happier, more comfortable and more confident.

It's the same with skiing; You need to relax and let go. Embrace the exhilaration of the mountain, welcome the sensation of freedom, and enjoy yourself. That's why you are there, after all.

Practice Visualization

Visualization is the number one technique used by sportsmen and women, elite businessmen and women, to take their performance to a whole new level, almost-effortlessly knock that fear out of their lives and become the person they most want to be. It's going to be one of the best tricks you can employ to take your skiing to a whole new level.

Best of all, it's absolutely free and you can get started wherever you are. Give the following three visualization techniques a go and witness the results for yourself.

ONE: Self-Observation Visualization

This visualization is all about watching your smooth and controlled descend down a short stretch of slope, but by doing it right there in your own head. Here's how to do it:

1. Close your eyes and see yourself in your mind's eye from a 3rd person perspective (as if you are outside of your body and watching yourself).

2. In your mind's eye, see yourself push off gently and ski a short distance before you come to a smooth and controlled stop.

3. As you do this, pay attention to the reactions that you are experiencing within your body. How are you feeling?

Are you tensing your muscles? Are you holding yourself awkwardly?

4. If you notice any stress-reactions, take the time to relax those muscles, breathe deeply and allow yourself to calm.

5. Repeat the process several times- my students often find 5 times or so is most effective.

TWO: Action Ski Visualization

This is much the same as the previous visualization, but this time you are going to experience the descent as yourself, from your perspective. If the fear factor isn't too strong for you, you can skip straight onto this visualization instead of practicing the former. The choice is yours! Here's how to do it:

1. Close your eyes and imagine that you are about to ski a short distance. See this from your own perspective. Make everything you can see as vivid as possible and allow all of your senses to experience where you are.

Smell the air, feel the cold air on your skin, be aware of the lingering taste of your breakfast, hear any sounds nearby; make it all come alive.

2. As before, see yourself push off gently and ski a short distance before you come to a smooth and controlled stop.

3. As you do this, pay attention to the reactions that you are experiencing within your body. How are you feeling? Are you tensing your muscles? Are you holding yourself awkwardly?

4. If you notice any stress-reactions, take the time to relax those muscles, breathe deeply and allow yourself to calm.

5. Repeat the process several times- again, five repetitions is usually about right.

THREE: Circle Of Confidence

The circle of confidence is a visualization which will allow you to revisit a state of confidence whenever you need to, whether that is during a skiing trip or in daily life when challenges come up. It's based on a technique which combines the power of visualization and another technique known as anchoring. Again, you can use this anytime. This is how it works:

1. Close your eyes and recall a time in your life where you felt extremely confident. Focus on it for a moment and remember exactly how it felt in your body. Did you have a rising sensation in your body? Did you feel as if the world was at your feet? Were you in complete control of your body?

2. Imagine you are right there right now, feeling all of the sensations throughout your body allowing it to spread throughout your body.

3. Now imagine a circle glowing on the ground beneath you, glowing at your feet. Tell me, what does you circle look like? What color is it? Does it have a smell? Is it moving? Does it carry with it a sound? Take the time to explore its details and make it as real as you possibly can.

Watch it grow and then when it's at its peak, step right out of the circle.

4. Now imagine yourself putting on your skis. That circle you imagined in the previous step is right there sitting on top of your skis, waiting for you. You step onto them and allow that circle to envelop you with the confidence you need to really make it happen. See it clearly, vividly, full of color, hear the sounds, make it all real.

5. Open your eyes and come back to the present, safe in the knowledge that you have the confidence and poise of a professional.

Find Your 'Why'

Why are you learning to ski? Is it to impress your friends? To become an Olympic champion? To bask in the sense of liberation and freedom that comes from sliding down a mountain? What is it?

When you narrow down your motivations for being on your skis on the first place, you also remember what is important to you, how much to push yourself and why. Because without that 'why', you will never find the inner drive to push yourself forwards and achieve great things on the slopes. You'll never exceed your own expectations and gain that sense of bliss that comes from fresh mountain air. What is your reason?

Fear and self-doubt are often the only factors that prevent you from taking your performance to an entirely new level. But you don't have to be victim to this turbulent master. Follow the steps in this chapter; allow yourself to surrender to the sensation, practice the visualization meditations and find your why. And you will be shocked by what you can achieve.

Chapter 5: Simple Exercises To Finely Tune Your Technique

All of the theory in the world can certainly help, but to get to the next stage, you'll need to get off of that chair and get moving. The following is a set of training tasks which you can do absolutely anywhere you like, in your living room at home, on your lunch break, in the staff room or even in the airport (although you might attract a certain amount of attention if you do it in the latter!)

They'll improve your technique and posture significantly, and also have a positive impact upon your overall ski fitness. I'd highly recommend that everyone work through the following exercises, even if they think their technique is pretty good. Doing so will iron out any creases and allow you to concentrate on the more challenging stuff. First we'll take a look at leg symmetry, then flex pattern, and finally dynamics. These exercises are thorough and as such, will take your time and attention. But they are absolutely worth it.

For best results, get a friend and a camera (still or video) to help you along the way and target your weaknesses.

Leg Symmetry & A-Framing

The most common problems that skiers face is that of unruly legs which just don't want to cooperate with their owners and stay in a parallel position, or that of A-framing, when the feet end up wider than the knees. Physiologically-speaking, our feet are naturally inclined to position themselves at a slight angle, so the majority of this really isn't any of your fault. Thankfully, with some attention and practice, we can overcome this tendency and get perfectly parallel legs.

TESTING

• Stand in your ski pose, with your entire body positioned at it is when you are actually skiing.

• Make 10 jumps from one side to another, capturing them with a camera or witnessed by a friend if you can.

• Check for your positioning during take-off, in the air, and whilst you land.

Feet Pulling Exercise

A great training task to employ is the feet-pulling exercise. By doing it, you'll finely tune your lateral leg control and keep foot symmetry in check

• Find a slippery floor such as one with a wooden floor or tiled surface.

• Place an item of fabric on the floor, such as a towel or t-shirt.

• Stand on the fabric with your feet around 80cms apart, and pull your feet towards a central point. Do this as slowly as possible.

Practice Symmetry

It's time to go back to the test jumps once again. To recap:

• Standing in your ski pose, with your entire body positioned at it is when you are actually skiing.

• Make 10 jumps from one side to another, capturing them with a camera or witnessed by a friend if you can.

• Check for your positioning during take-off, in the air, and whilst you land and aim to continuously control your leg positioning. This is harder than it sounds, but it's worth getting it right.

RE-TEST

It's time to go over your recent camera images with a friend and check your progress. If you've improved vastly then you should be proud of yourself. If you still need work, rest now but return to the exercises at a later date.

Tackling Your Flex Pattern

A poor flex pattern will put your body weight on the back of your skis, increasing your chances of falls or injury, as well as posing a greater strain on your muscles and causing you to look amateur. The secret is to learn to flex comfortably on the balls of your feet, reduce your knee flex and increase your ankle flex. Here's how to troubleshoot this issue.

TESTING

- Stand in your ski pose, with your entire body positioned at it is when you are actually skiing.

- Make 10 jumps from one side to another, capturing them with a camera or witnessed by a friend if you can from the side, paying close attention to your flexing of the ankle and knee.

Be aware of your ankle flex

There is no easy shortcut to this one- you'll need to increase awareness and action of your ankles if you want to improve. The simple way to do this is to assume your test jump position and try to land as quietly as you can whilst maintaining good position.

Be aware of your knee flex

Stop sitting back and instead position yourself forward until your weight is resting on the balls of your feet. Your thighs should be driving down on top of them and your thighs should be as vertical as you can make them.

RE-TEST

It's time to go over your recent camera images with a friend and check your progress. If you can see that your body is more centered and you create less noise when you land, then you have made a great difference. Over time, muscles memory will make this posture effortless.

Dynamics

Do you want more leg lean when carving, or more of a dynamic launch when changing direction? You'll need to practice the following exercises which will allow you to improve in these specific aspects, even if you are thousands of miles away from the nearest patch of snow.

TESTING

This section of exercises is all about pushing your limits and moving towards new goals. The way we get started on this is to mark your current jump limitations right there on the ground beneath you. As with the previous exercises, jump from side to side paying close attention to the points we raised in the previous exercises. Mark the distance you've covered on the floor with chalk markings or even electrical tape.

Train

Practice each one of the exercises you have learned in the previous sections, aiming to improve your performance and distance. When you've worked out how to optimize your airtime and launch, pay attention to the angle of your legs whilst you're in mid-jump. They should swing underneath your hips into a well-angulated position with the upper body. Allow yourself to land again and repeat. This will help you to react efficiently at higher speeds, allowing you to tackle more challenging trails and gradients.

These three training focuses will allow you to iron out any problems you might be having, and directly improve your performance even if you aren't anywhere near a patch of snow. In actual fact, practicing these things at home gives you the edge and allows you to get a substantial head-start if skiing is an activity you only participate in for a fortnight or two per year.

In this chapter, we have covered the finer details and now we are going to get extra-physical by taking a look at the precise strength training exercises you need to target those often underused ski muscles. This not only improves your performance but also helps you to stay out there enjoying the experience for longer. We'll also take a look at the importance of cardio and how you can use it to boost your abilities. Come and find out how.

Chapter 6: Strength And Cardio For Skiing

Skiing is an intensive activity for the human body, and so even if you know where to place your limbs, the right angles, the correct posture, and every other technique in the book, you're going to fail at the first hurdle if you are unfit. You'll tire more quickly, you'll run out of breath, your muscles will tire, and yes, you'll put yourself at a far greater risk of injury. Clearly, this means that if we are seeking success on the slopes, it's vital that we pay adequate attention to our strength and fitness, and more specifically, our ski fitness.

This chapter will help you boost that fitness, leaving you ready to take on the world without your body letting your down. We'll include cardio tips and strength-building exercises which will help you feel awesome. Let's take a look.

The Importance Of Strength

Awesome skiing isn't just about being an expert of posture, positioning, technique and balance- your strength and physical fitness pay an enormous role in your success or failure when you're out there. Because you can possess all of the skill in the world, but if you tire too easily, you'll have to quit before the rest and never make all of your dreams become reality.

However, fitness and strength is often the least appealing element of ski preparation, as it feels as if it has little to do with the sport itself. Yet with a well-designed short sequence of exercises and an active lifestyle, you can make all of the difference before you even leave home.

The main areas you need to work to improve your skiing are your core, your leg strength, hamstrings, hips and ankles. To ensure balanced fitness and overall healthy, we'll need to balance this will an additional focus on flexibility and cardiovascular health.

The Exercises

The following seven exercises will target each of the most important muscles groups and help them support your skiing experience. Try to practice them at least three times per week for at least 30 days prior to your skiing holiday, or even longer if time allows. Don't forget that these exercises aren't only to be used for skiing- they'll keep you strong and ready for action all year round, so make them part of your fitness regime wherever you can. Enough of the talk- let's get started.

Ski Squat

The ski squat is the quintessential ski exercise which recreates your leg motion when you are riding more difficult trails. Here's how to do it:

• Stand on one leg in a ski stance. Place your other foot onto a chair behind you.

• Squat down until your leg is at a 90-degree angle. Keep your knee strong and avoid allowing it to move in either direction.

• Raise to standing, then repeat 12 times.

• Take a moment or so to rest, and then repeat for three sets.

• You should be feeling a burn in your thigh muscle which shows you that you are targeting the correct muscles. If it's all too easy, consider holding weights if you need to. In the gym, use dumbbells, or at home choose whatever you have to hand.

Basic Lunge

This exercise strengthens the muscles on your outer and inner thigh and also improves strength and flexibility in your knee, hip and ankle joints. Here's how to do it:

• Stand with your legs hip width apart, your hands resting on your hips.

• Start with your left leg and take a large step forwards until your back knee touches the floor. Then return to your starting position, and repeat on the other side.

• Complete 3 sets of 15 repetitions each.

• Again, you will feel quite a burn in your glutes and quads- this is a great sign that you are working the correct muscles.

Walking Lunge

This exercise uses the same principle as the basic lunge, but instead of returning the starting position, you back leg moves forward to join your front leg. This is how it works:

- Stand with your legs hip width apart, your hands resting on your hips.

- Start with your left leg and take a large step forwards until your back knee touches the floor.

- Then bring your back leg to meet your forward leg, and repeat on the other side.

- Complete 3 sets of 15 repetitions each.

Plyometric Lunge

The plyometric lunge is the most challenging of the lunge series and employs your explosive muscle action to really train up your ski skills and improve your muscle fiber reactions. Here's how to do it:

- Stand with your legs hip width apart, your hands resting on your hips.

• Start with your left leg and take a large step forwards until your back knee touches the floor.

• Push up from the floor until you are standing with your legs straight- one in front and one behind.

• Quickly switch feel so the opposite foot is in front.

• Now repeat the same thing using this leg, and then switch again.

• Complete 3 sets of 15 repetitions each.

Hamstring Curl

Your hamstrings play a vital supporting role to the whole of your leg, including your knees, and as such protect against knee and muscle injury. This exercise helps to strengthen these muscles whilst also engaging your core. This is how to do it:

• Lie on the floor flat on your back and place both feel onto a yoga ball/physio ball.

• Keep your arms at your sides to help you balance.

• Now comes the fun bit! Lift your butt off of the floor, and using your core muscles, pull the ball towards you several inches, until your feet rest comfortably on the top of the ball.

• Roll back to your starting position and take a deep breath.

• Repeat the exercise, doing 3 sets of 15 repetitions.

'Clam' Exercise

The clam exercise is often forgotten when it comes to ski training, but it's important to include in your pre-ski workout as they target the outer butt muscles which are often difficult to work. Here's how to do it:

• Lie on the floor on your side with your hips and knees bent as if you are skiing.

• Keeping your legs parallel to the floor, lift your upper leg as high as you can whilst maintaining effective body position, and return to the floor.

• Repeat this exercise 15 times, resting when you feel the burn becoming too intense.

• Shift onto the other side and repeat 15 times on the other leg.

Plank

It's vitally Important to have good core strength in order to make skiing easier and help you cope with the intense pressure you will feel when making turns. This increases tenfold as you tackle more challenging terrains and higher speeds. If your middle is too weak, you will collapse under the pressure and are more likely to do yourself some damage. Here's the perfect exercise to streamline your core:

• Get down onto the ground and lie on your stomach.

• Place your elbows directly under your shoulders with your arms straight out in front of you, palms flat on the floor.

• Using your abs and glutes, lift your hips off the ground until your back forms a straight plank shape.

• Hold for 30-60 seconds, depending on your fitness

• Repeat 5 times.

Flexibility & Cardio

As I mentioned earlier, you'll want to pay attention to your flexibility and cardiovascular fitness too. This will support your body to perform at it's absolutely best, and will also improve your overall health. You can target these things in whatever way you want, better still if these are things that you love. Why not try the following ideas?:

Cardio

- Interval training

- Cycling

- Running

- Athletic swim training

- Skipping

Flexibility

- Dynamic stretching

- Yoga

- Pilates

In this epic chapter, you've learned all of the precise exercises you can do to target those essential muscles that you most engage when you take to the slopes. Incorporate them into your workout and you will notice your confidence, technique and power explode.

We've covered a lot of information in this book so far so congratulations for making it this far. Our final chapter will take everything we've learned into consideration and wrap it all up with some final tips that will take you from your current ski levels to those of your dreams. Let's take a look.

Chapter 7: Everything Else! Final Advice For Confident Skiing

We've packed a ton of information right into this book so that you can really take your skiing to a whole new level. However, there are still several additional tips I'd like to offer you before we wrap things up. They are those things which don't fall into any particular category yet will also make a difference to your performance, including tips on making the most of your performance and tricks to push yourself forwards in your skiing career.

Watch The Professionals

As you might know, a little inspiration goes a long way when it comes to sport, so indulge in your passion through the supreme skill of others. You'll be surprised just how much it rubs off. So as much as you can, watch as much skiing as you can, whether that's in person, on television or on YouTube. The latter is a great on-tap resource that will allow you to discover amazing new tricks at the touch of a button. Just enter the name of your favorite champion into the YouTube search and voila, amazing inspiring skiing. If you've yet to get stuck in the world of the pro, try out one of the following names:

- Didier Cuche

- Ted Ligety

- Lindsey Vonn

- Lara Gut

- Bode Miller

- Daniel Albrecht

- Hermann Maier

- Aksel Lund Svindal

- Michael Walchhofer

- Ivica Kostelić

- Marco Büchel

Push Yourself

Aim to ski with others who are slightly more advanced than you are. This will push you to attempt things that you might not otherwise, and therefore take greater leaps towards improving. However, do make sure you keep safety in mind at all times and know your limits.

Set Yourself Goals

You'll need a roadmap in place if you ever want to improve your confidence and skill. So take the time to consider your goals, outline them carefully and then take the steps to move towards them. Throughout your journey, monitor your progress so that you can review your progress. Make sure these goals are both realistic and easily achievable.

Video Yourself

To understand your own strengths and weaknesses better, record your own performance. This technique is popular amongst elite sportsmen and women, and will also help you. It's also a good way to monitor your progress as you move towards those goals that you just outlined.

Have Fun!

All work and no play will definitely make us all dull boys and girls. So smile, have fun and remember why you started skiing in the first place.

Be Positive

Don't get too hung up on your weaknesses. Instead focus on the positives and use these to build your confidence on the slopes. You'll be amazed at the improvement this will witness from doing just this.

Adjust Your Technique

Remember that you will need to adjust your technique depending on the conditions and also the terrain itself. This becomes especially important as you move up the skiing ranks.

Ski More Frequently

The only way you can improve over the long-term is to spend more time on the slopes. So get out there and get skiing!

Take Care Of Your Body

Make sure you are well-rested, hydrated and nourished at all times, and pay close attention to your self-esteem and confidence. Do this and your skiing will take care of itself.

The tips you have just learned are the icing on the top of the skiing cake. And the best bit of all is that you get to eat the metaphorical icing. Along with the rest of the information you have learned in this book, use this information to give you that winning edge that you are looking for. Sometimes it's the smaller tips that make the most difference, so don't forget to give them a try too.

Final Words

Before you read this book, you probably thought that moving from being a mere beginner to really gaining confidence on the slopes was going to take a huge expense, multiple trips to the slopes every year and plenty of sweat and tears along the way. And I'll be honest with you- you'll never improve your skiing performance and confidence overnight.

But with the right training techniques, most effective visualization techniques, strength and fitness advice and precise exercise that I have included for you right here in this book, you will improve quicker, faster and most cost-effectively than you would ever expect. There's no doubt in my mind that you will utterly surprise yourself the next time you take to the slopes.

Your level of skill and confidence comes down to just one person: you. Only you can make the improvements you desire, only you can make your skiing dreams become reality. When you have finished reading through this book, make a plan to really put the steps into action. You can only get better by physically doing, and not just learning the theory.

Get out there, enjoy your skiing experience, and never lose sight of the bigger picture!

[1]http://www.wired.com/2014/02/ski-run-nyman-sochi-olympics

[2]http://www.ncbi.nlm.nih.gov/pubmed/10198142

13403790R00032

Printed in Great Britain
by Amazon